William Bolcom

From the Diary of Sally Hemings

Eighteen Songs for Medium Voice and Piano

Text by Sandra Seaton

ISBN 978-1-61774-251-4

EDWARD B.
MARKS MUSIC
COMPANY

EXCLUSIVELY DISTRIBUTED BY

HAL•LEONARD®
CORPORATION

7777 W. BLUEMOUND RD. P.O. BOX 13819 MILWAUKEE, WI 53213

www.ebmarks.com
www.halleonard.com

Commissioned by Music Accord, Inc., a consortium of presenters, including the Boston Symphony Orchestra at Tanglewood; the Chamber Music Society of Lincoln Center in New York; the Fortas Music Series of the John F. Kennedy Center for the Performing Arts in Washington, D.C.; the Krannert Center at the University of Illinois in Urbana; the Library of Congress in Washington, D.C.; the Ravinia Festival of Highland Park, Illinois; San Francisco Performances; and the University Musical Society, University of Michigan at Ann Arbor.

The World Premiere of *From the Diary of Sally Hemings* took place on March 16, 2001 at the Coolidge Auditorium, Library of Congress, Washington, D.C. by Florence Quivar, Mezzo-soprano and J.J. Penna, Piano.

The work is recorded on compact disc by Alyson Cambridge, Soprano and Lydia Brown, Piano on the label White Pine Music (WPM221) released in 2010.

TABLE OF CONTENTS

to the memory of Flournoy Miller

From the Diary of Sally Hemings
PART ONE
I.

SANDRA SEATON

WILLIAM BOLCOM
(2000)

N.B Accidentals obtain throughout a beamed group. Unbeamed notes within a measure continue the same accidental until interrupted by another note or rest. In music with key signatures, traditional rules apply.

voice:___ Sal - ly, keep this bell, pray for your dear

sis - ter. The mas - ter, tall,

straight back bent in grief, swore___ he'd nev - er wed a -

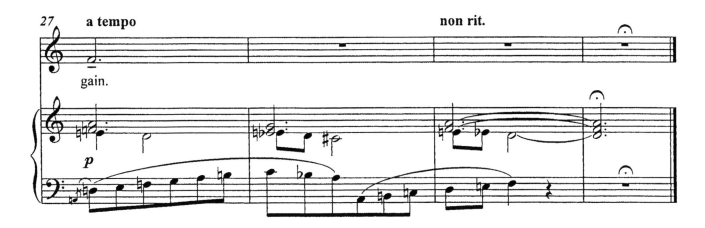

gain.

II.

Lively, rhythmic (♪=132)

Mar - tha and Ma - ri - a, hands clasped to - geth - er

in the shade of his pop - lar tree, we skipped and stopped, spied his

a little slower

words on her grave:_____ *If in the house of Ha - des, men for - get their*

a tempo

dead, *yet will I re - mem - ber my dear com - pan - ion.*

Most days I sit with Ma - ri - a and Mar - tha, her quill rest - ing in my palm, a

spy in an - oth - er coun - try. In - side, the big house.

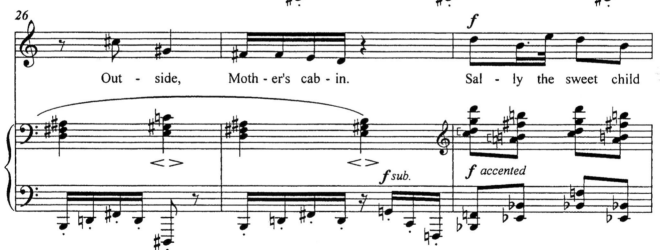

Out - side, Moth - er's cab - in. Sal - ly the sweet child

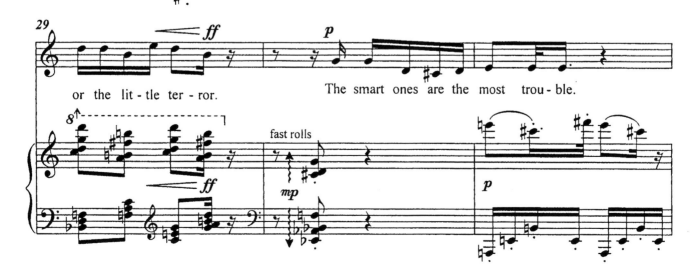

or the lit - tle ter - ror. The smart ones are the most trou - ble.

Here, Mar - tha, let me hold the book. We'll pre - tend.

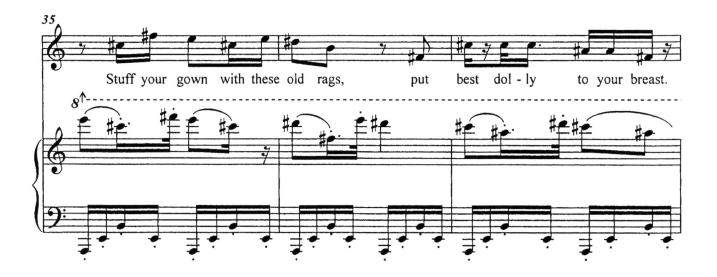

Stuff your gown with these old rags, put best dol - ly to your breast.

Like so.

III.

8

quietly rhythmic (♩=62)

Da - ho - mey child,_____ be - troth - ed___ when she was

young, a prin - cess be - fore she knew of white men or the

sea, she knew the___ ways of___ home.   A

thin veil of fog. Her fam - i - ly brings a farm - er, a

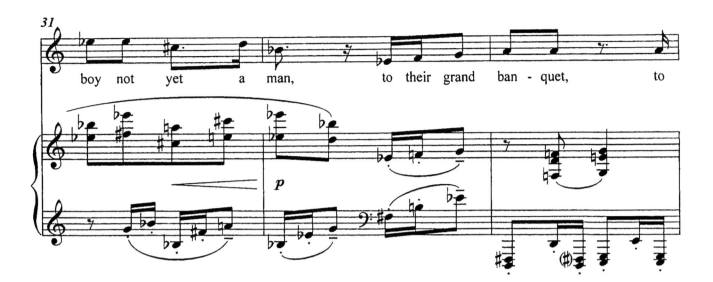

boy not yet a man, to their grand ban-quet, to

mar-ry with the busi-ness of the home._____ Each dawn she

poco agitato

climbs the palm tree to touch the wine__ with her hands. A feast pre-

a tempo

pared,   the Gods must have a   hand   in this: a   young goat,   sac - ri - ficed,

cresc.   **f**   **mp**

o - kra,   or - ang - es,   a bas - ket of yams   laid at her feet.   She stands in the

midst of old   friends,   clothed in new fin - e - ry,   bu - ba and i - ro____   of an odd - col - ored

rit.

blue,   hair in beads, piled to the sky,   tap - ping the palm wine from the

in the blue - black sea.   Now a voy-age of a dif-ferent sort.

Ma - ri - a would-n't go___ un - less I came a-

long.___   White waves___ in the blue - black

poco rit.

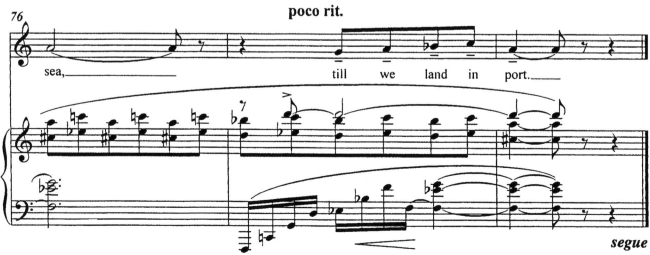

sea,___   till we land in port.___

segue

IV.

* French pronunciation

Jef - fer - son wants things just so. A young wo - man

must dress pro - per - ly. Not a wrin - kle nor a speck of dirt.

If I break an - oth - er dish, I won't have to wash the

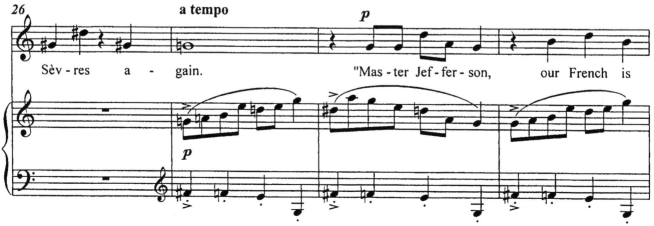

Sèv - res a - gain. "Mas - ter Jef - fer - son, our French is

poor. Those words we learned back home, a girl's French,

poco rit. **a tempo**

they don't work here." The

French tu - tor comes to our vil - la. I hur - ry a - round,

a piacere, cantando

dust - ing the room. Then I stop, pick up the book, cop - y the

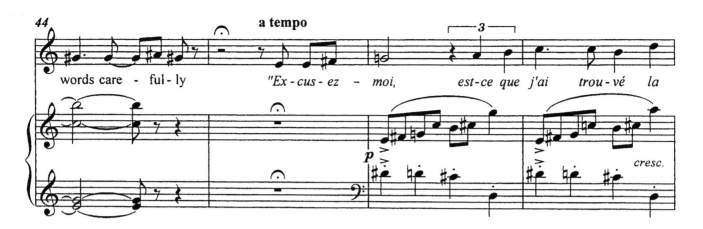

words care - ful - ly   "Ex - cus - ez - moi,   est-ce que j'ai   trou - vé la

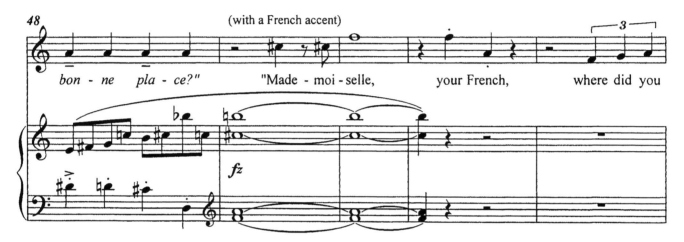

bon - ne   pla - ce?"   "Made - moi - selle,   your French,   where did you

learn   that?"   "Was I not   ex - pect - ed to know?"   "Where did you

learn   your French?"   "At the   big house,   where else?"—

Stir-ring the sauce, add-ing the cream, re - duce by

half. Fort bien. Cham - pag - ne Pois-

son, a mar-vel-ous sauce. C'est for - mi -

da - ble. Ra - ge de Par - is.

18

V.

fi - ne." On our morn - ing walk when the men___ bow, his pos-

ses - sive - ness keeps___ me safe._____ Comme d'ha - bi -

tu - de, first one ser - vant boy, then an - oth - er, they fol - low me when

Mas - ter Tom leaves. On his re - turn, he finds me

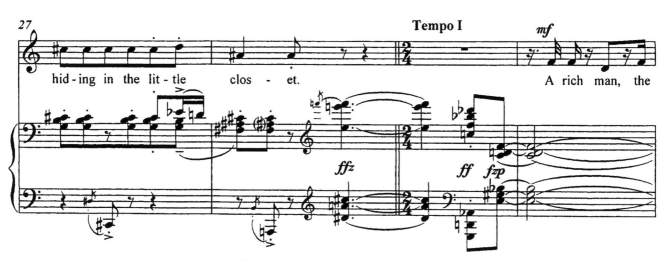

hid-ing in the lit-tle clos-et.

Tempo I

A rich man, the

Mar-quis de Brail-les,* of-fers him gold for me. "Il est trop**

più agitato

(approximate pitches)

en-tre-pre-nant." Mas-ter Jef-fer-son flies in-to a hor-ri-ble rage.

Fast

Tempo I

p (ironically)

short

"Elle est charm-ante et fi-ne."

short

short

no Ped.

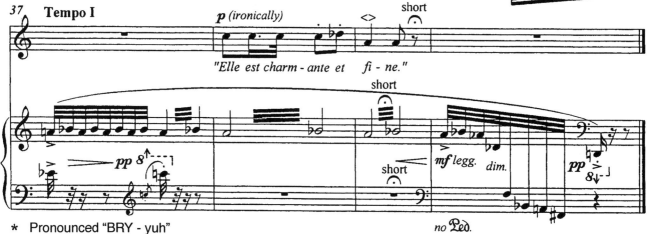

* Pronounced "BRY - yuh"

** Please use the "p" in the liaison to the next word.

VI.

ev - er was.   He   cupped my face in his hands

and   whis - pered her name.

PART TWO
VII.

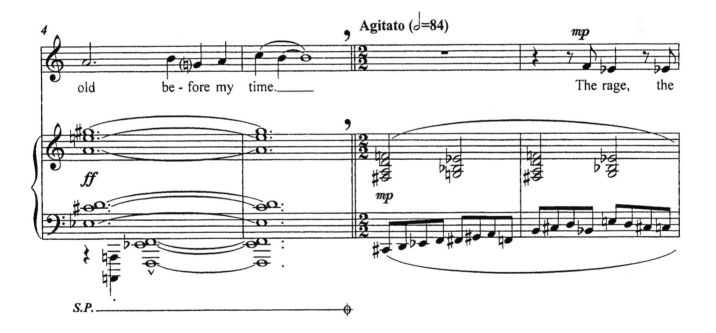

24

* pronounced "Ba-STEE-yeh."

26

VIII.

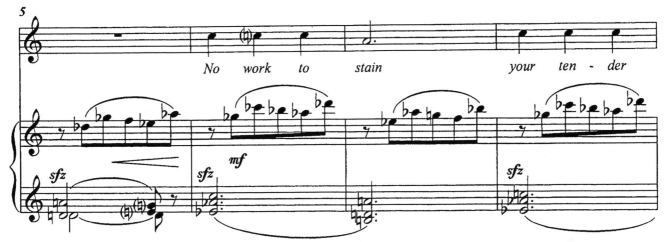

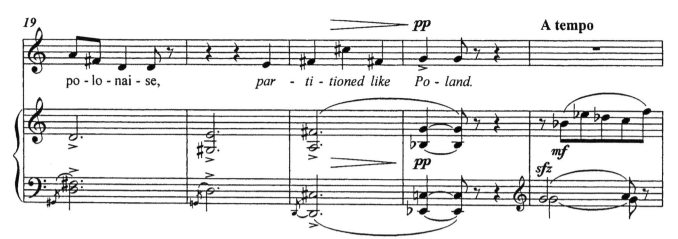

po - lo - nai - se, par - ti - tioned like Po - land.

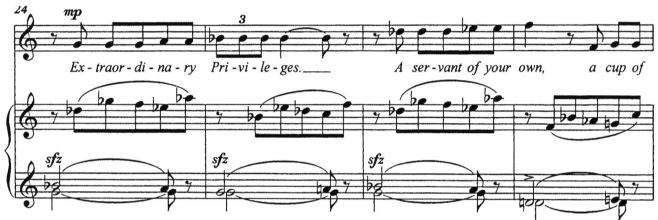

Ex - traor - di - na - ry Pri - vi - le - ges.___ A ser - vant of your own, a cup of

broth, a plate of Mar - seilles figs at dawn. I said no.___

——— Then he took to his sick - bed, six

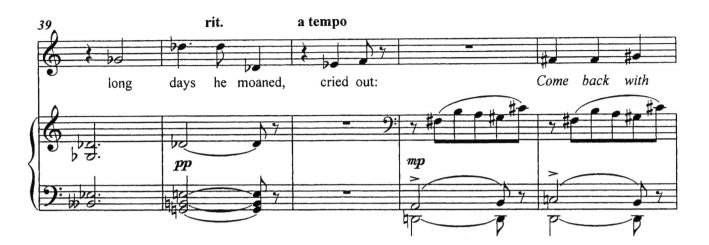

long days he moaned, cried out: Come back with

me. Bri - oche en cou - ron - ne. Your own pen and

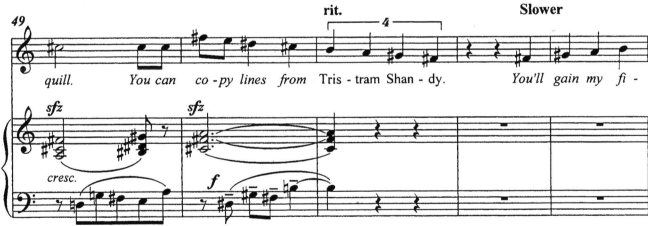

quill. You can co - py lines from Tris - tram Shan - dy. You'll gain my fi -

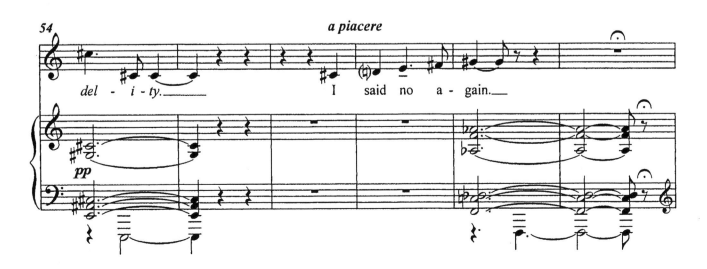

del - i - ty.____ I said no a - gain.____

When I said yes, we packed bags for A-

mer - i - ca, set sail with two cork oak trees,

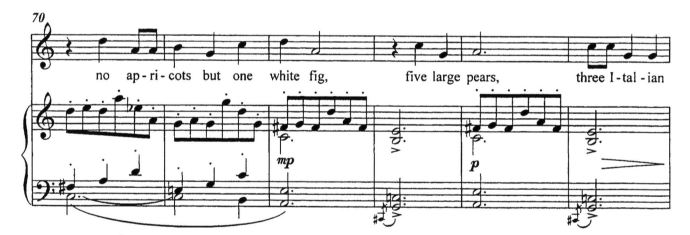

no ap - ri - cots but one white fig, five large pears, three I - tal - ian

pop - lars, and u - ne robe à la fran - çai - se.

IX.

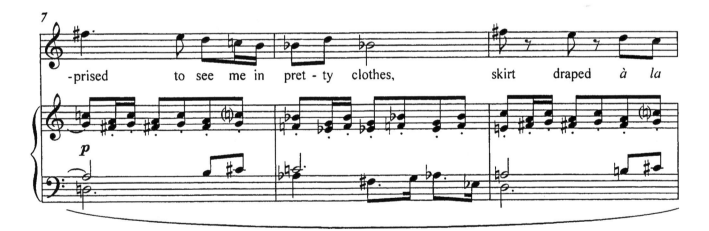

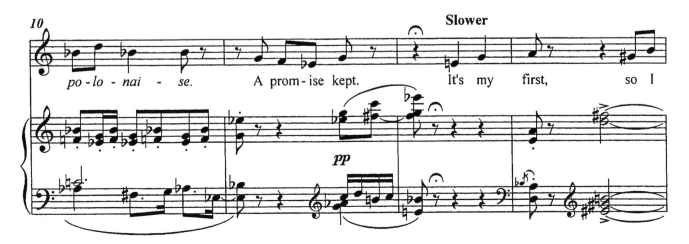

don't show. *Elle n'a pas l'air.* Till Moth - er puts her

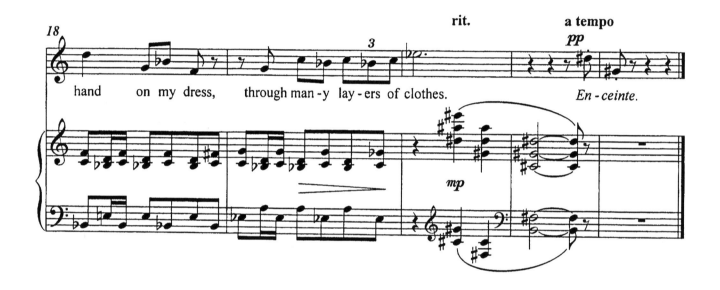

hand on my dress, through man -y lay -ers of clothes. *En - ceinte.*

X.

Tenderly (♩=80)

Pur - ple Hy - a - cinth be - gins to bloom.___ A-

lone in his sanc - tum sanc - to - rum, I call him Mis - ter. No wom - an goes

there but me.___ I am in charge of his cham - ber, a po - si - tion of pow - er,

three lit - tle rooms with a wall of seeds, his king - dom in a small clos - et, a

garden la - beled and hung in per - fect or - der.___ Yes - ter - day I

found five plums.___ I have a room of my own, in that room I am a

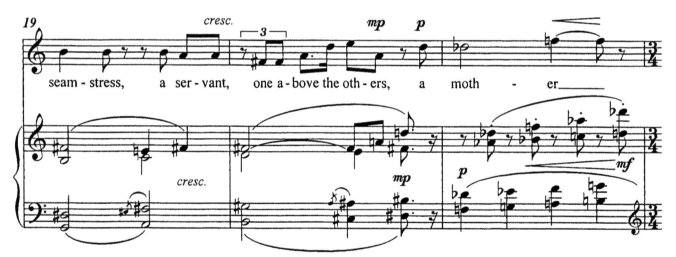

seam - stress, a ser - vant, one a - bove the oth - ers, a moth - er___

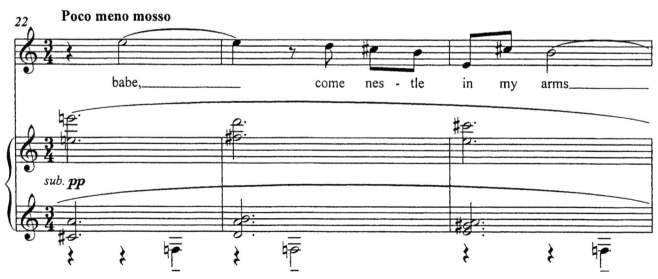

Poco meno mosso

babe,___ come nes - tle in my arms___

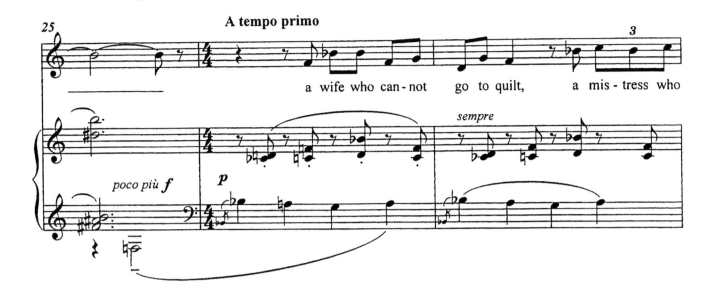

XI.

Rich and Warm (♩=46)

mp

My sis-ter ghost, rath-er

me than a strang-er who__ rules__ her own king-dom. Rath-er

me__ than a strang-er. Blood-lines!

Moderato (♩.=76)

A la-dy__ dress-es pro-per-ly__ from the ear-li-est mo-ment of the

p very smooth and even, very slight accents

sempre

l.h.: *no accents*

day. With im - pec - ca - ble man - ners he gives me a lec - ture on how to dust a

book: *Hold the feath - er dust - er to the book.* *No, like so.*

Place your hand on mine here.__ *First the cov - er, firm but*

not too firm.__ *Dust the pag - es, then the rim.*

poco agitato — A little slower

32

Now, smooth the sheets, spread the bed.

Then he ar-

p sub.

pp sub.

A tempo

36

ranged my hair on the pil - low.

mp

cresc.

f

Lively (♩=120) rit.

40

One day I called him Tom. He turned, star - tled:

f

mf — f

Tempo of VI (♩=69)

44

3

Now hold your face towards the light.

He held me close.

pp

p

u.c.

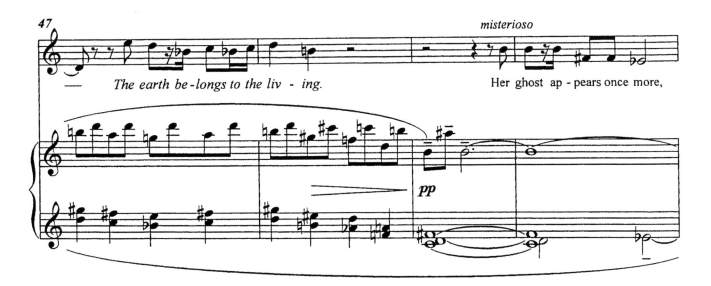

The earth be-longs to the liv - ing.

misterioso

Her ghost ap - pears once more,

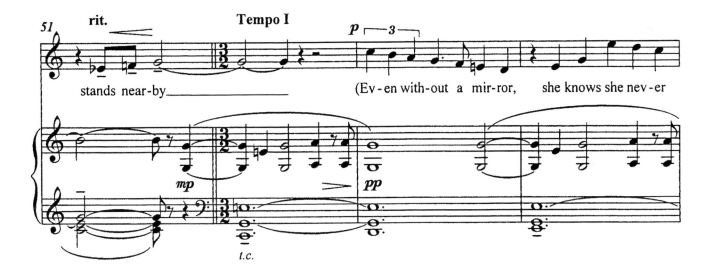

stands near-by_____

(Ev - en with-out a mir-ror, she knows she nev - er

had my looks.) Sis - ter dear, I hold your daugh-ter's trust. Rath - er me than a

40

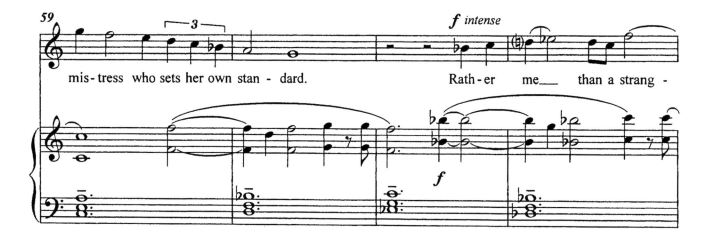

mis - tress who sets her own stan - dard.   Rath - er me___ than a strang -

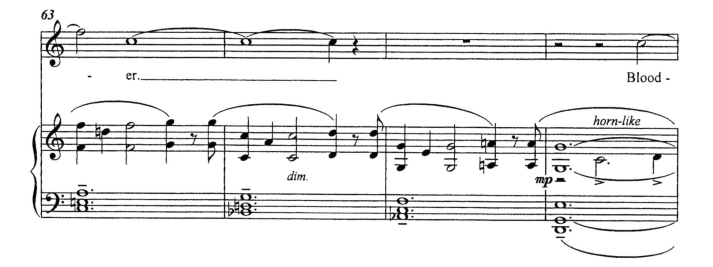

- er._____   Blood -

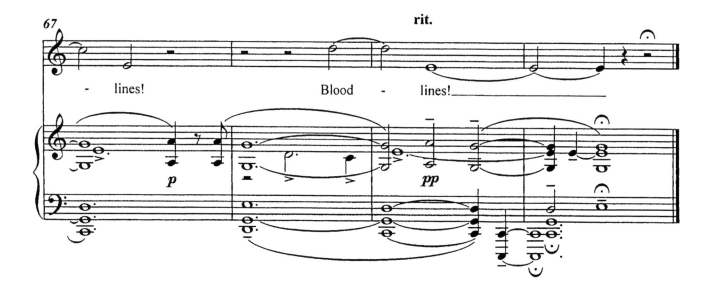

- lines!   Blood - lines!_____

PART THREE
XII.

*Use the damper pedal to make *diminuendo*; release pedal and retake chord silently.

book, two blot-ters, one scope, pow-der for my hair — o - ver there.

What's the lit-tle one do-ing with my book? Mis-ter, I'm read-ing it to him.

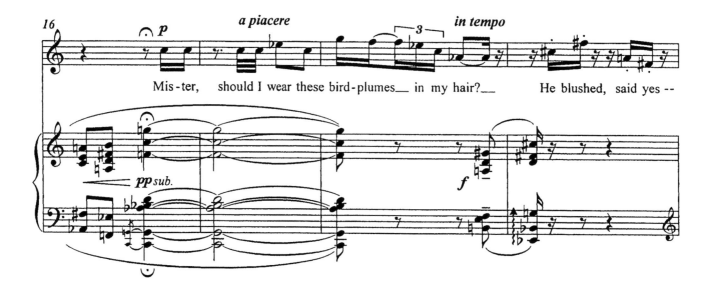

Mis-ter, should I wear these bird-plumes__ in my hair?__ He blushed, said yes --

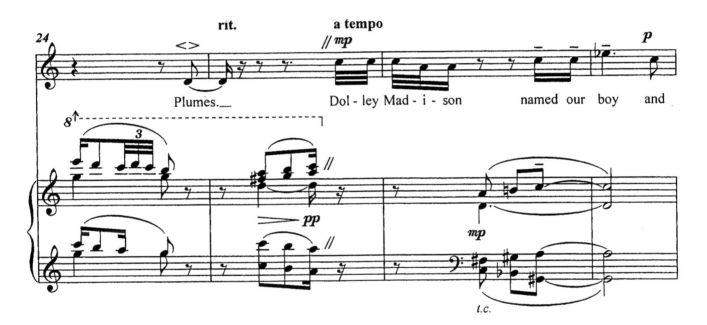

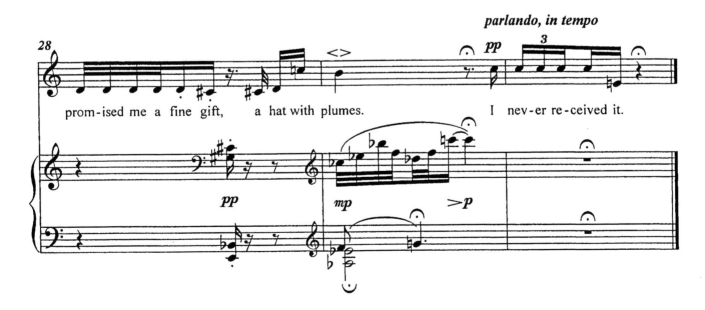

XIII.

Slow, bleak (♩=69)

Mis - ter, our child is frail._ This time pray with me.__ Pray_ she has strength. Glo - ry be to

God. Ho - san - na__ in the high - est. An - oth - er babe gone._

No soon - er had I fin - ished nurs - ing her__ than she left my arms.__

XIV.

-toiles   with her grand *bal-lon* that reached the sky,_____   who walked a - long-side the

Duc de Bris-sac,   car-ry-ing her jew-eled fan?   In her silks and her pearls she ad-vis-es the

Duc on af-fairs   of state.   Mis - ter!   Where are all the kings and queens?

XV.

Old shoe! Old shoe!

He fid-dles for the chil-dren,

for me. Taught the boys to read and write, though we can't ad-mit it.

Did the boys___ learn their les-sons? Mad-i-son, stand still. Bow___ for Mis-ter

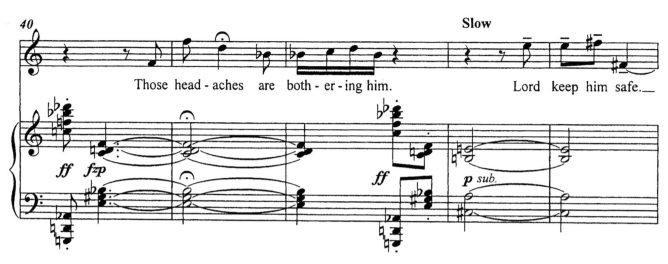

Those head - aches are both - er - ing him. Lord keep him safe.—

Oh! Mis - ter! ear - bobs___ all the way from

Phil - a - del - phi - a. I'll wear them well. There's been___ no oth - er

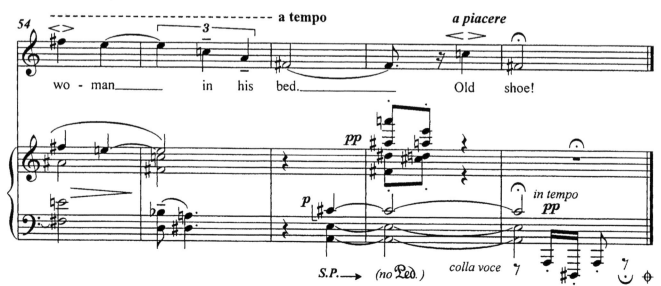

wo - man___ in his bed.___ Old shoe!

PART FOUR
XVI.

Murmuring, restless; tempo of I. (♩=66)

p

u.c.
very little 🮲.

A wild man home from the woods. Se-

vere weath-er has killed most of the fruit. When he's

like this, he has to do some-thing. He's tear-ing up the

house a - gain. The dust, his head - aches. Heav- en - ly

fa - ther, he's wear-ing his old brown coat and socks that don't

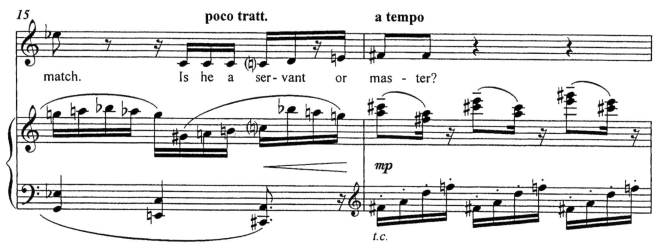

match. Is he a ser - vant or mas - ter?

Smooth the bed, spread_ the sheets,

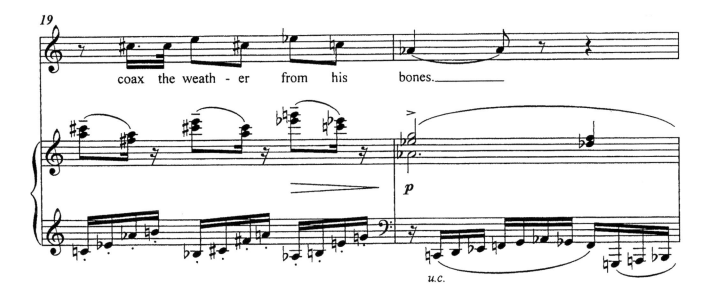

coax the weath - er from his bones.____

u.c.

meno mosso

If in the house of

mf

t.c.

A tempo primo

Ha - des,   men for - get their dead....____

La vie noc - turne à Par - is.   To

rit.

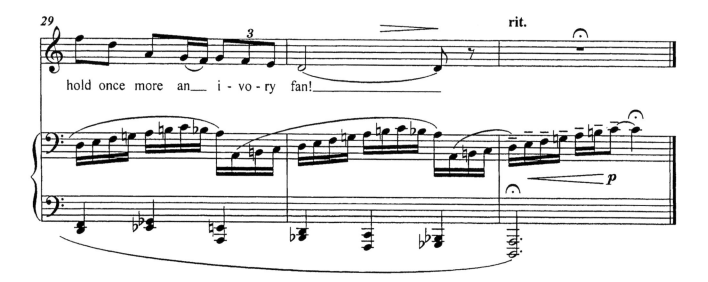

hold once more an__ i - vo - ry fan!____

XVII.

clutch-ing a   thin gold   cross.

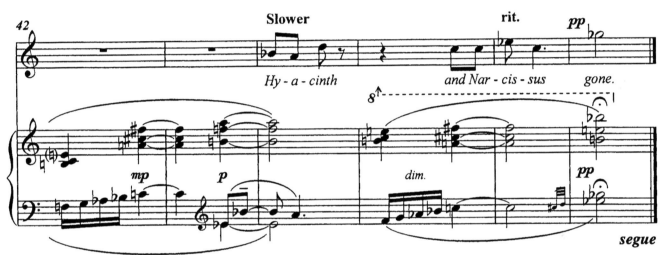

Hy - a - cinth   and Nar - cis - sus   gone.

segue

58

XVIII.

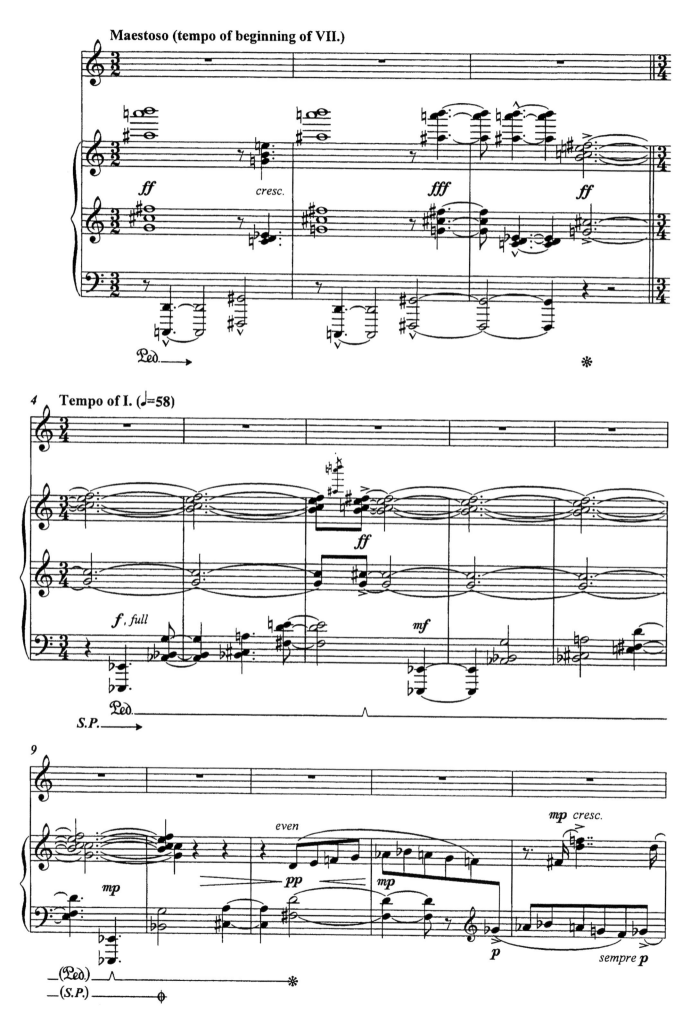

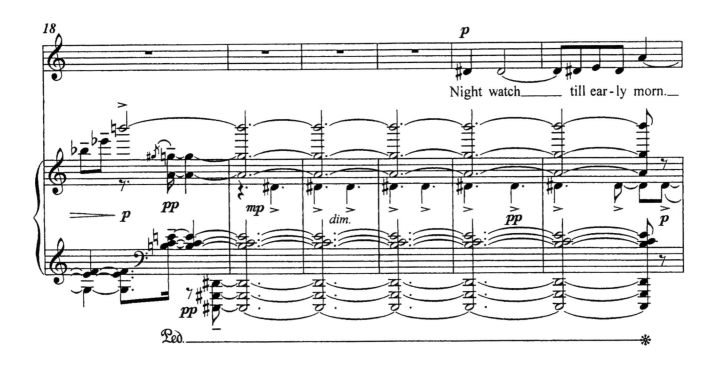

me._____ I left our pil - low   by your side.___

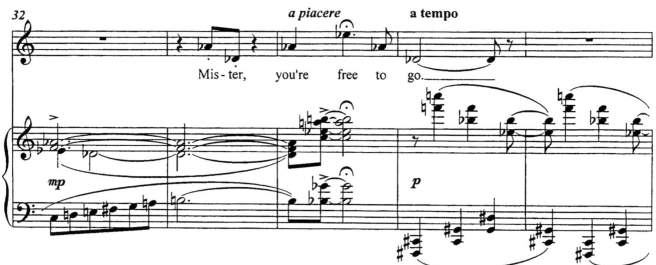

a piacere   **a tempo**

Mis - ter,   you're   free   to   go.___

Lay   out   the   trou - sers, Press   the coat. Starched lin - en   shirt and col - lar bears his

fine em - broi - dered vest.   No pow - der for his   hair.   A touch of rib-

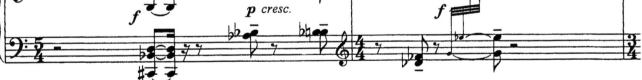

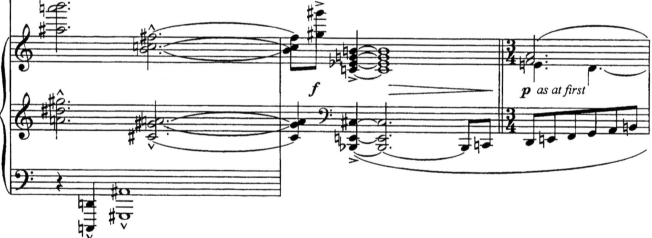

This time walk with me___ to the Lord. We'll dress in our new

fin-er-y,___ silk robes___ to meet___ our__ Lord.

Note: Thomas Jefferson's spoken words are in italics, as are quotations from his writings. To distinguish Jefferson's own words from those of Sally Hemings or other speakers, no other words are italicized, including French phrases.

PART ONE
I
They say I was born old, so so old before my time. I stood by mother, under the canopy bed, saw Mistress Jefferson raise four fingers. I was nine years old. Heard Mother's voice: Sally, keep this bell, pray for your dear sister. The master, tall, straight back bent in grief, swore he'd never wed again.

II
Martha and Maria, hands clasped together in the shade of his poplar tree, we skipped and stopped, spied his words on her grave: *If in the house of Hades, men forget their dead, yet will I remember my dear companion.* Most days I sit with Maria and Martha, her quill resting in my palm, a spy in another country. Inside, the big house. Outside, Mother's cabin. Sally the sweet child or the little terror. The smart ones are the most trouble.

Here, Martha, let me hold the book. We'll pretend. Stuff your gown with these old rags, put best dolly to your breast. Like so.

III
White waves. A century gone. My mother's mother in the lower deck. Wet and cold in the blue black night, I dreamt a bitter dream:

Dahomey child, betrothed when she was young, a princess before she knew of white men or the sea, she knew the ways of home. A thin veil of fog. Her family brings a farmer, a boy not yet a man, to their grand banquet, to marry with the business of the home. Each dawn she climbs the palm tree to touch the wine with her hands. A feast prepared, the gods must have a hand in this: a young goat sacrificed, okra, oranges, a basket of yams laid at her feet. She stands in the midst of old friends, clothed in new finery, buba and iro of an odd-colored blue, hair in beads, piled to the sky, tapping the palm wine from the palm tree. Kidnapped before the roast meat was cold, snatched away to America, she was a stranger to the sea.

White waves in the blue-black sea. Now a voyage of a different sort. Maria wouldn't go unless I came along. White waves in the blue-black sea, till we land in port.

IV
Paris, c'est la ville vivante. Men call me beautiful, une vigne sauvage. Skin white, whiter than white, near white. From the first moment of the day, Master Jefferson wants things just so. A young woman must dress properly. Not a wrinkle nor a speck of dirt. If I break another dish, I won't have to wash the Sèvres again.

"Master Jefferson, our French is poor. Those words we learned back home, a girl's French, they don't work here." The French tutor comes to our villa. I hurry around, dusting the room. Then I stop, pick up the book, copy the words carefully. "Excusez-moi, est-ce que j'ai trouvé la bonne place?" "Mademoiselle, your French, where did you learn that?" "Was I not expected to know?" "Where did you learn your French?" "At the big house, where else?"
Stirring the sauce, adding the cream, reduce by half. Fort bien. Champagne Poisson, a marvelous sauce. C'est formidable. Rage de Paris.

V
The master brings music to his sitting room, a fine harpsichord to soothe his head. His pain is my own.

The grand dukes and their duchesses, they say "elle est charmante et fine." On our morning walk when the men bow, his possessiveness keeps me safe. Comme d'habitude, first one servant boy, then another, they follow me when Master Tom leaves. On his return, he finds me hiding in the little closet.
A rich man, the Marquis de Brailles, offers him gold for me. "Il est trop entreprenant." Master Jefferson flies into a horrible rage.

"Elle est charmante et fine."

VI
I was carrying a tray when he called me. *Sally, turn this way. Now hold your face to the light. A little over.* Master Jefferson looked whiter than a sheet, whiter than I ever was. He cupped my face in his hands and whispered her name.

PART TWO
VII
They say I was born old, so so old before my time.

The rage, the anger, épouvantable! The sound of thunder. Tear down the gate! Throw off the chains! Another traitor sent to hell. Storm the Bastille! Effrayant, the light of lightning. Girl, you've been here before. Safe in his arms, but still my voice frightens him.

VIII
Come back to America. No work to stain your tender hands, the run of the house. Your own gloves, gowns, robe à la francaise, skirts draped à la polonaise, partitioned like Poland. Extraordinary Privileges. A servant of your own, a cup of broth, a plate of Marseilles figs at dawn. I said no.

Then he took to his sickbed, six long days he moaned, cried out: *Come back with me. Brioche en couronne. Your own pen and quill. You can copy lines from Tristram Shandy. You'll gain my fidelity.* I said no again.

When I said yes, we packed bags for America, set sail with two cork oak trees, no apricots but one white fig, five large pears, three Italian poplars, and une robe à la francaise.

IX
Back home at Monticello, I step out of the carriage. Oh, they're so surprised to see me in pretty clothes, skirt draped à la polonaise. A promise kept. It's my first, so I don't show. Elle n'a pas l'air.

Till Mother puts her hand on my dress, through many layers of clothes. Enceinte.

X
Purple Hyacinth begins to bloom. Alone in his sanctum sanctorum, I call him Mister. No woman goes there but me. I am in charge of his chamber, a position of power, three little rooms with a wall of seeds, his kingdom in a small closet, a garden labeled and hung in perfect order. Yesterday I found five plums.

I have a room of my own. In that room I am a seamstress, a servant, one above the others, a mother--babe, come nestle in my arms--a wife who cannot go to quilt, a mistress who shares her household, who holds a daughter's trust. The next best thing. *Purple Hyacinth and Narcissus bloom.*

XI

My sister ghost, rather me than a stranger who rules her own kingdom. Rather me than a stranger. Bloodlines!

A lady dresses properly from the earliest moment of the day. With impeccable manners he gives me a lecture on how to dust a book: *Hold the feather duster to the book. No, like so. Place your hand on mine here. First the cover, firm but not too firm. Dust the pages, then the rim. Now, smooth the sheets, spread the bed.* Then he arranged my hair on the pillow.
One day I called him Tom. He turned, startled: *Now hold your face towards the light.* He held me close. *The earth belongs to the living.*

Her ghost appears once more, stands nearby. (Even without a mirror, she knows she never had my looks.) Sister dear, I hold your daughter's trust. Rather me than a mistress who sets her own standard. Rather me than a stranger. Bloodlines! Bloodlines!

PART THREE
XII

Peonies, a perfume box. *Wild Honeysuckle still in bloom.* Quadroon. Octoroon. Mixing colors in a vase. The orderly and the insignificant. A list? Yes, your orderliness. *The garden book, two blotters, one scope, powder for my hair.* Over there. *What's the little one doing with my book?* Mister, I'm reading it to him. Mister, should I wear these bird-plumes in my hair? He blushed, said yes–a little music please.

Plumes. Dolley Madison named our boy and promised me a fine gift, a hat with plumes. I never received it.

XIII

Mister, our child is frail. This time pray with me. Pray she has strength. Glory be to God. Hosanna in the highest.

Another babe gone. No sooner had I finished nursing her than she left my arms. God rest her soul. Keep her safe.

Did I tell you, Lord? Martha's child had a fine funeral, gloves passed out by the hundreds, buried in the family plot. Not like my Baby Harriet.

XIV

A dark winter blue-black evening, la vie nocturne.

Mister! Do you remember a Madame So-and-So who did not wear her jewelry well or arrange her hair? And the Madame d'Étoiles with her grand ballon that reached the sky, who walked alongside the Duc de Brissac, carrying her jeweled fan? In her silks and her pearls she advises the Duc on affairs of state.

Mister! Where are all the kings and queens?

XV

Old shoe! Old shoe! He fiddles for the children, for me. Taught the boys to read and write, though we can't admit it. *Did the boys learn their lessons?* Madison, stand still. Bow for Mister Jefferson. Old shoe.

They say let a man have his ways. Make a little home. Don't question him when he goes away, so they say.

A letter from Washington, with cotton stockings wrapped in tissue. A little note: he misses me in the morning. Those headaches are bothering him. Lord, keep him safe. Oh! Mister! Earbobs all the way from Philadelphia. I'll wear them well. There's been no other woman in his bed. Old shoe!

PART FOUR
XVI

A wild man home from the woods. *Severe weather has killed most of the fruit.* When he's like this, he has to do something. He's tearing up the house again. The dust, his headaches. Heavenly father, he's wearing his old brown coat and socks that don't match. Is he a servant or master? Smooth the bed, spread the sheets, coax the weather from his bones. *If in the house of Hades, men forget their dead . . .* La vie nocturne à Paris. To hold once more an ivory fan!

XVII

Papers! I've never seen so many. When I come in, he hides the news. *Cancel all the papers. Do you hear me? Let no man break this bond.* Sworn to secrecy.

Old shoe! Be rid of me. You'll save your name. Mister, take this part, the part that was my sister's, my soul.
Our son Beverly ran off. And Harriet was sent away in a carriage, clutching a thin gold cross.

Hyacinth and Narcissus gone.

XVIII

Night watch till early morn. Smooth the sheets. Spread the bed. No need to send for me. I left our pillow by your side. Mister, you're free to go. Lay out the trousers, press the coat. Starched linen shirt and collar bears his fine embroidered vest. No powder for his hair. A touch of ribbon near his slippered feet. No need to hide the news.

At dawn her ghost appears. Do I covet, Lord? She never had my looks. Night watch till early morn. I dare not sleep lest the ground grow wild. If I take my freedom, come and go, Old Shoe, will you pursue me still? No room for me in your graveyard. A servant in my place.

Morning glory! A little house with my darling sons. Madison says I'm pining away. Round back, I hear Tom keeping time for Eston, fiddler, fiddle, fiddle, string! Do I dare disturb their bond?

At dusk her ghost returns. Plumes in her hair. He lies with her in his sanctum sanctorum. A hedge of willows marks their sitting room. *"No sound to break the stillness but a brook . . the feeble ray of a half-extinguished lamp . . ."* Blue-black evening, la vie nocturne. I'll come to tend your grave. But you'll sleep, you'll sleep with sister dear. Crave me.

Dear children, his letters, my diary, this picture with his name, strike every word.

I was born old, so old before my time. Once I went off to see the world, sailed across the sea, longed for a pouf à la circonstance, a crown to touch the sky.

Mister, we're free to go. Leave your old clothes behind. This time walk with me to the Lord. We'll dress in our new finery, silk robes to meet our Lord.